From Crack Cocaine to Christ From Calvary

From Crack Cocaine to Christ From Calvary

✦

The true story of an addicted man's rehabilitation through Christ JesusThis book is for the broken spirit that is struggling in ANY addiction and looking for an open doorway out!

Minister Anthony M Love Sr.

This book is for the broken spirit that is struggling in ANY addiction and looking for an open doorway out

iUniverse, Inc.
New York Lincoln Shanghai

From Crack Cocaine to Christ From Calvary

The true story of an addicted man's rehabilitation through Christ JesusThis book is for the broken spirit that is struggling in ANY addiction and looking for an open doorway out!

iUniverse books may be ordered through booksellers or by contacting:

iUniverse
2021 Pine Lake Road, Suite 100
Lincoln, NE 68512
www.iuniverse.com
1-800-Authors (1-800-288-4677)

The views expressed in this work are solely those of the author and do not necessarily reflect the views of the publisher, and the publisher hereby disclaims any responsibility for them.

Edited by Debra Taylor

ISBN: 978-0-595-43985-0 (pbk)
ISBN: 978-0-595-88306-6 (ebk)

Printed in the United States of America

I'm writing this book to honor God for what He has done in my life.

This book is dedicated to my wife, Lisa M. Love, my parents Anderson and Rosa Love, my children Tyesha, Candice, Anthony Jr., Michael, and Samarra, my grandchildren Joey, Taylor, and Gabriel, my Grandmother-in-law Alice W. Jones and my cousin Timothy Washington.

Also, this book is written in loving memory of my brother Ira S. Love, my mother-in-law Barbara C. Carter, and my cousin Calvin Washington. God Bless you all for everything.

Introduction

Upon reflection of my life, I have experienced the lows one person can inflict upon himself, and the Higher Power of God that can lift him out. I have discovered the truth that His love is trustworthy for those that believe and have faith in His Son Jesus Christ as our Redeemer and Healer. It is my most sincere prayer that those that read the pages of my life's journey know that with God, all things are possible to those that put their hands into the hands of the Savior. For many years, I could not understand why the Lord would allow me to go through what I chose to make of my life, but His Word says, "All things work together for good." (Romans 8:28), and my situation did indeed work together for good. I want to share my experiences with those that are hurting in their bondage of addiction to let them know that Christ is the light at the end of their tunnel as He was at the end of mine. May God open your heart to him as he opened mine.

I was raised in a low middle class neighborhood in Camden, NJ in the 1960's. It was a peaceful and serene life, a typical safe childhood. I would step into a neatly designed row house setting with flowered lawns front and back, at Halloween, our street looked like acres of children running from door to door in multi-colored costumes. We had the finest parents any child could want; they were very loving and giving. Christmas time was spent in the neatly furnished living room of our home with gifts piled in five different sections. It was peaceful, our parents watching as we opened our gifts one by one.

I am the fourth of five children, my oldest sibling and only sister Teresa, my oldest brother Anderson, Ira, myself, and my baby brother Rodney. Even though we had many neighborhood pals, Rodney and I were like best friends, doing everything together, mischievous in our own way as typical boys are. Anytime something was broken in the house, our father would always yell RODNEY! TONY! COME HERE! We were always picked out first, even if we didn't know anything about the situation. I had an excellent dad, stern, and meant what he said. I remember the first time my dad used the "F" word; he was very angry that someone had broken into our storage garage behind our house. It really shocked me because that kind of language was not used inside or outside our house.

My dad worked for the No. 1 radio station in Philadelphia, driving a 45 minute commute each day. We met many entertainers like Stevie Wonder, the Jackson Five, and Gladys Knight and the Pips. Some entertainers would even come over, like a group called the Mad Lads. One day, they and my dad fell asleep at our house, tired from performing and traveling. One of the group members was sitting in my dad's recliner wearing silk socks. He had a large bill stretched out inside his socks to be purposely displayed. I don't remember the exact denomination, but it was a large bill. I thought it was a cool thing to do. I still do it myself from time to time. This shows theinfluence one person can have on another.

At a very young age, I started working at the radio station during summer vacation, doing odd jobs, like cutting the grass or cleaning the offices, to make extra money. Drugs and alcohol were never talked about in our house, but I remember one of the first times I was exposed to it. One of the DJ's was smoking marijuana on the air. It was burning in the ash tray, and I knew it was something bad, but it had no effect on me at that time.

My dad worked at the radio station for 21 years and I've never had anyone from there directly mislead me to do wrong. It was just the environment that was a high to me. In those days, many children admired the Love boys, and I knew we had a life many children only dreamed of. Time went on, and when I was 12 years old, my parents announced we were moving to the suburbs of East Mt. Airy in Philadelphia. The fear of moving from quiet Camden, NJ (in those days) to the fast paced life in Philadelphia was so great that I insisted to my mom that she allow me to take karate lessons. I began my lessons in 1972 and was very successful in them.

I was 14 years old when the trouble started with my arrogance. The marijuana faze was already sweeping through the black community, and it seemed everyone was doing it but me. Ira was the fast one out of all my siblings. He was into the night clubs, parties, tailor made clothes, drugs, and rock and roll. Ira was a guy a lot of boys envied, not knowing his lifestyle of drug use, as he was very secretive about it. He would do his dirt behind a tightly sealed door so the rest of the family didn't find out. While Anderson was into fancy cars and had tons of girls, Teresa was trying to find her own way in this dark and dying world. Rodney tried to imitate Ira after a while by wearing three-piece suits and other fashionable clothing. There came a time that I discovered Rodney had been smoking joints (that is what we used to call it). He was more open to dysfunction than Ira was. I criticized Rodney for doing what it seemed he and everyone else was doing, but I still continued to develop my fighting skills. I was later turned on to speed pills that we street named 'christmas trees'. It gave me so much energy, I could do twenty repetitions curling a dumbbell, when previously, I could only do ten. I had sense enough to ease off of it because I came to the realization that I could hurt myself or have a heart attack.

We were all raised going to church, even before we moved to Philadelphia, but were never told or taught the sheer reality of Jesus Christ (Romans 1:19-20). I remember once, I was in the bathroom of our six bedroom single home that God began to reveal to me a sense of life and death and I've never forgotten it. He revealed to me in my spirit that we are all going to die some-day. This thought and revelation came out of nowhere and this was the first of many visits of the Lord speaking to me in my spirit.

My karate teacher in those days was my cousin who was four years older than me. He had a black belt and the swiftest kicks I've ever seen in person, and I wanted to fight just like him. He taught me very well, so well that I wanted to be under his wing al the time. I eventually discovered that he smoked marijuana, and I just had to try it along with him. I got so high that when we took the three mile walk home, I felt like I was a robot walk-ing down the street. That day opened the door to my path of self destruction. I believe I was instantly addicted.

Because of karate and throwing my weight around, as my mother used to say, I was sixteen years old and three years behind all of my classmates in high school. I remember my mother telling me "Tony, you're not going to live long if you don't get that chip off your shoulder". To have my loving mother tell me that was a rude awakening for me. I was a jerk! I thought no one could beat me at fighting. My dad was an ex-boxer, and I thought I could take everyone on, even him. I remember one day, I balled up my fist because he was chastising me for something I did wrong. He hit me first, and the next thing I knew I was knocked into the hallway from the living room. I never tried anything like that again with him, but the arrogance continued. At school, I started drinking, smoking joints and skipping class with my best friend J. R. (Jay) Wilson and others. I was terrorizing other children in school using my fighting ability and I remember a girl writing in my junior high yearbook "Don't smash everyone you meet".

In 1977, on the last day of school, I met a girl who was to become my wife. She was fifteen and I was seventeen. Eight months later, she became pregnant with our first child, Tyesha, the light of my life. I would take her almost everywhere I went, high or not. I was never one to be a stumbling drunk, but boy did I drink and smoke. I would wake up in the morning and drink straight vodka. All along, I was still being lied to by the devil. He would tell me that it wouldn't affect my fighting ability which meant so much to me. I became physically abusive to my wife, due to my arrogance, and the continued use of drugs and alcohol. I was openly running around with other girls, and would become abusive when I would come home late and my whereabouts where questioned.

We moved in with the cousin that taught me karate and his wife. He was also physically abusive with his wife, so I thought it was ok to be that way towards mine. My cousin and I got along fine. During the short period of time we stayed at his house, he and I never argued or fought. Once, he came into our bedroom and said if we heard fighting between he and his wife, not to worry about it. We moved after a few months because I found an apartment. It was rented to us by a con artist who didn't really own the property, but I wasn't aware of that at the time. I was eighteen years old then, and stayed home drinking and smoking joints all day, picking up odd jobs occasionally. It was convenient, with the liquor store only two blocks away, and a pint of vodka only costing $2.25, my so-called friends and I would drink all day, everyday. Through leading a dysfunctional life with my young wife and children, we moved around several times until we ended up renting a room in the basement of my parents house, back in Mt Airy.

One day, I was high and arguing with my wife, when I threw a cup at her as hard as I could, just missing her head. When I turned back around, she had snuck out of the house for the fourth and final time to go back to live with her parents. She refused to return to a life of drugs, alcohol, abusiveness and hell. The separation devastated me so much that I developed a gastric ulcer from worrying and drinking on an empty stomach. We had been together five and a half years.

Six months later, on December 18, 1983, I met Lisa, who would become my second wife. Our relationship began with both of us using drugs and alcohol, which was leading us down a road filled with torment and misery. I had graduated to snorting cocaine and meth and I slowly stopped training and fighting. I was twenty four years old and I would do speed and stay up twenty four hours or more full of energy working around the house, drinking and smoking cigarettes. My wife Lisa would snort cocaine and smoke cigarettes occasionally, but I did it like I needed it to live. Three months after we met, she became pregnant with my third child. I had two girls with my first wife, and my second wife gave me my first son, something my first wife wanted very much to give me.

After she became pregnant, Lisa stopped doing drugs and smoking cigarettes, just like a wet towel hitting the ground. Nine months later my son, my junior, was born. When he was about a year old, I smacked Lisa during an argument, and she moved out. I couldn't find her for a month, but eventually found out that her mom rented an apartment for her about 10 miles away. I talked her into returning home with the promise of never hitting her again. I knew I would lose her like I did my first wife if I didn't change my ways. We had a little two bed-room home in the Germantown section of Philadelphia and my life seemed to be turning around for the better. Lisa's mother and grandmother hated the very ground I walked on because I had persuaded her to return and because of the lifestyle I was exposing her to. I did slow down with some of my destructive habits; I furnished our home, bought a used car that I custom-ized myself, bought my mother a nice used car, and had a full time job.

I began to hang out with a war veteran that lived two doors down. He could purchase all the meth you wanted and that opened the doors to more demons sent in by satan himself to destroy the prospective servant of God I was called to be. I had gotten to the place in my existence that being high was being sober and being sober was being high, because I was used to being high all the time. With the power of God foreseeing my future, He would enable me to keep a full time job, with my employers barely able to tolerate my tempers and arrogance, while trying to hide my addictions. I recall a time when I was arrested on a bench warrant for overdue traffic tickets. They held me for two days and nights, and while in custody, all I could think about was how to get out and get to the half ounce joint on my night table, wanting desperately to get high.

While living in Germantown, I met a lady around the corner from where Lisa and I lived. She introduced me to freebased cocaine, formed with baking soda. The high was good to me, but didn't really move me until one day when I was about twenty-seven years old.

I was on an outing to North Philadelphia to purchase powdered cocaine, and was introduced to crack cocaine which was sold in a tall vial and sealed with a bright yellow cap. I was amazed at how much I would get in one vial and I would smoke tiny little rocks that would last me all day for only five dollars. Later in life, I realized it was the lure of the devil to pull me in. He came as an angel of light (2nd Corinthians 11:13-14) because the first high was the best feeling I had ever had in my life. I thought the feeling was even better than sex.

I took my first hit inside my blue camaro a half block from where I purchased it. I didn't get addicted immediately, it took about a week. Some people get hooked or addicted their first time, but satan reeled me in slowly until he pulled me out of the water of semi-consciousness and put a choke hold on my life. He had me good, he finally had me good! I started to drink less liquor too. I was down to about two or three six packs of beer a night after work, a case on Saturday and a case on Sunday. I would sometimes buy two five dollar vials after work and by the time the night was over, I would have spent one or two hundred dollars and have to face the morning with sorrow, poverty and regret.

There were times when I would buy a TV for my family, paying one hundred fifty to two hundred dollars for it, and the next morning I would hand it out the window from my first floor apartment to one of my fellow crack addict cohorts to sell for twenty five or thirty dollars. I would pass it out the window while my wife and young sons were playing in the front yard. They would come into the house shocked to see a small black and white TV or no TV. Anything of value I would pawn or sell. I remember once being out until four in the morning trying to sell a TV that was barely worth ten dollars, which I never did sell. That was when I knew within myself that I was truly a drug addict. For thirteen years, I was locked in the grip if the devil's darkness.

My dear sweet brother Ira was overcome by the snares of the evil one. One day in January of 1992, Ira passed away after he contracted AIDS from intravenous needles. Meanwhile, Rodney continued down the same road that leads to the untimely death of your body and soul.

My parents moved out of their six bedroom house in Mt. Airy to a one bedroom apartment because of their two remaining addict sons constantly returning home after failing in the world. With their large house, we didn't worry about failing because we knew we had some place to go. Rodney was given a house in the Olney section of Philadelphia which was ultimately turned into an undercover crack house. After my parents moved, my wife and I moved into the house also, we had very few expenses but we still struggled to meet them. We had ice cold water to wash the dishes and bathe with and no heat in the winter. Around this time, Lisa decided she couldn't take it anymore and left unexpectedly, moving to southwest Philadelphia to live with her dad, because of the way in which I chose to provide for my family. My oldest daughter, who had come to stay with us briefly after a fallout with her mother, also left unexpectedly.

I continued to get high and kneel in the palm of satan. One night the temperature outside dropped to five degrees below zero, I was heating the curtained off bedroom with 2 kerosene heaters and one electric heater. Even with 5 blankets, it was like sleeping outside due to the poor insulation of the house. It was only through the Grace of God that I didn't freeze to death that night. I haven't been that cold before or since that night. Another day in the same house, I had a Doberman Pinscher that someone had given me for protection because of the poorly secured house. One day, as I sat alone on the bed, the dog was sleeping on the floor a few feet away. All of a sudden, the dog looked up and put his tail way down and bolted out of the room, seemingly for no reason. To this day, I believe he felt or saw the presence of evil in that house. By the Grace of God, I was still holding a full time job, though I don't know how anyone put up with me. After we lost the house to sheriffs' sale, we lived briefly in a garage that we heated with a kerosene heater. We had to turn it off and open the door every half hour to air the garage out. I would wake up every day with dozens of empty crack vials on the burned night table, spending my hard earned money to destroy my life. I attempted suicide twice. The first attempt paralyzed my right side after I took a half bottle of aspirin (about twenty tablets). The second time, I cut my wrist four times, bleeding everywhere, yet somehow, God sustained me. I cried many nights because of the hell I chose to make of my life. I cried tears because satan would not let me go free.

Rehab was a joke to me. I came out worse than when I went in. All along, Christ was kneeling on the door of my tortured soul saying "I am the way, the truth and the life" (John 14:6). I remember a session in rehab when a guy stood up and said if you don't like someone, you don't have to kill them, just give them a hit of crack cocaine. That was one of the biggest truths I've ever heard. Later in my addiction, God sent me a mentor who was a Church leader and prominent politician that ministered the word of God to me and stuck by me throughout my rehab days. His name was E. Randy Urquhart and the Word he delivered never left my spirit. I remember he recommended I praise and thank God for everything by saying "Thank you Father, thank you Jesus, thank you Holy Spirit". This man stood by me through thick and thin, but I insisted on living the life I chose and he faded from my life.

Crack is a selfish, agonizing, and destructive substance which holds the same characteristics of satan who comes to kill steal and destroy (John 10:10). Satan influences the mind of man to lead our soul into hell; he invents ways to pull man from the love and peace that God truly wants us to have. The Bible calls satan the god of this world (2 Corinthians 4:4) because more people choose to follow him down his dark road (Matthew 7:13-14).

Throughout my addiction, I've seen many lives destroyed. I remember one guy that waited years for a lawsuit to be settled. He didn't work because of the suit, while his wife did all she could to sustain the family which included four or five children. He would spend some of their welfare money to get high on crack, and I remember him telling me that when he got his money from the lawsuit, he was going to take care of himself and no one else, and that's exactly what he did. When he finally got his thousands of dollars, he bought a new car and smoked himself to death in a matter of 3-4 weeks. His wife ended up getting the car and the rest of the money. His sister-in-law told me that his heart had exploded. They say God don't like ugly and He sure proved his point.

Crack cocaine is an addiction that causes a person under the influence to be self centered, paranoid, untrustworthy, a chronic liar, and easily enticed to do evil. I know because I developed all of these characteristics. It will make you do things you would never do or think of when you're sober. Crack cocaine has a demonic force that speaks to your mind to use,

steal and lie. It will lead a person to jail, insanity, death and ultimately, hell. With crack, you are very conscious of your actions,
very conscious; you are just highly compelled to do wrong. All
through my addiction, I always believed in a living God, but the
evils of the drug seemed to consciously keep me from Him (2
Corinthians 4:4). Christ was working through me as well as in
me. I know this because almost anytime I needed to find or
know something from the Bible; I would amazingly go right to
it. That doesn't happen now though, the Lord makes me work
for what I am looking for. There was a time near the end of my
addiction that I would tell myself "I will not get high today, I
WILL NOT." I would sit and watch TV with my wife, laugh-
ing and playing, and then the spirit of the drug would make its
appearance. "Tony, Tony, buy one, just one, it'll be okay."
Every time it wasn't okay though, I would lie, steal, and borrow
all night long until the spirit was satisfied it once again had me
defeated, spiritually, mentally, and financially.

One day in 1994, I owed a drug dealer money and didn't
have any intention of paying it. My goal that day was to buy a
couple of five dollar vials. Three dealers asked me for ten dollars. I said I didn't have it and insisted on paying them later.
They turned aggressive and came toward me wanting to do me
bodily harm. All of a sudden, out of my mouth I shouted the
name Jesus! They walked away like the shield of Christ all of a
sudden covered me, and I never did get high that day.

Those of you reading this that have a problem with addiction, always remember through good times and bad, call on the

name of Jesus. There is power in His name. Satan has every intention on killing the user in his addiction. I remember telling my wife on some of my 3 AM drug runs on my bike (sometimes riding with a flat tire), "Lisa, I am very high, keep me in mind while I am gone." I never actually voiced it, but I was telling her tokeep me in mind in case I never returned home. Satan hates God because he knows he is eternally lost, and he knows we have something he'll never have, a chance for salvation. For that, he hates us, and devises every kind of destructive behavior to destroy us and our eternal soul whether it is drugs, alcohol, sex, pornography, or gambling. Anything he can think of to separate us from the life Christ so desires to give us, including eternal life with him. Christ comes so we can have life and have it more abundantly (John 10:10).

A crack addict has no life; it is an existence, a sinful miserable existence. Even when you're sober, it is just a sinful, miserable existence because you dread the next crack calling and the outcome of it. There is no comfort or 'so called' problem escape in this addiction. It ultimately destroys your health, marriage, children, employment, reputation, finances, and soul. Some say you aren't hurting anybody by using, but that's not true. You're hurting you and everybody and everything associated with you. It will never balance out, only decline and decay. Another way crack cocaine is damaging to your health is it strongly overrides your bodies' symptoms to any illness and makes you feel better than you actually are. It makes you susceptible to pneumonia, heart attacks, high blood pressure, strokes and death.

There was a time when I would smoke the drug and my heart rate would increase. I would lie down, put a piece of paper on my chest and watch how fast it moved. I would actually be worried, but continued to get high. Crack cocaine also increased my beer consumption, because it seemed to level off the paranoia and anxiousness caused by the drug. All the while I did this not realizing my liver and kidneys were being affected.

An addict will always be lied to by the enemy. He will tell you there is no light at the end of your tunnel and you'll never stop using. Satan is a master deceiver (Isaiah 14:12-15). Christ IS the light at the end of the tunnel. He will never leave us nor forsake us (Hebrews 13:5-6). Seek Him and you shall find, knock and the door will be opened (Luke 11:9). The Bible tells us that Satan is the father of lies (John 8:44), it also tells us that Jesus is the way, the TRUTH, and the life (John 14:6). If Christ says knock and it will be opened, then it WILL be opened, but YOU must walk through. He tells us to seek and we will find. He doesn't say He will seek for us. We must seek for ourselves. He tells us to put on the full armor of God (Ephesians 6:14), He doesn't say he will put it on for us. He supplies the armor; WE have to put it on. Looking back at the characteristics of the Triad, where Jesus says He is the Way, the Truth, and the Life, for our hope and destiny, He is the way to the Father, he is the way to Joy and Peace on earth, he also says He is Life eternal for us to obtain now and it can only come through Jesus Christ our Savior. God manufactured human beings and supplied us with an owner's manual, which is the Bible. If we choose not to follow it, we will destroy our life and our way to live with the Father and Savior forever (2 Thessalonians 1:8-9). The world holds no other books, doctrines or scripts for a GUARANTEED loving, joyful, and peaceful life on planet earth. Anything but the Word of God is imitation, deception, and false hope. The Word of God says all scripture is given by inspiration of God (2 Timothy 3:16). Jesus says if you're not for me, you're against me. Like I said previously, I've always known of God and believed in a living God, I just chose not to follow Him, and that left the door open to all kinds of demonic spirits until I chose to ask God to cover me with the shed blood of our Redeemer, and walk through the door that Christ said He would open. I was bought back with the price that had been paid at Calvary. What a faithful God! He's true to His promises and covenants that he will never break by any means. Throughout the sixteen years of my crack cocaine addiction and twenty-seven years of alcohol, I never had peace or solitude within myself. I never had security or hope for a future or love for my fellow brethren until I allowed Christ to come into my heart. That security, hope and love automatically came out from my heart, and showed in my actions without conscious trying on my part because Jesus is in charge and now lives in me.

I was inspired and asked by my dad to write this book because he is so awed at how Jesus turned my life around and the results of what Christ has done for me that I could not do for myself. As a result, my parents, oldest brother and his wife and four of my five children have dedicated their life to Christ. I trust God to draw in the fifth child, and the salvation of many more with the testimony I was given to share.

I've come a long way in the eight years since I've been saved. I didn't know how to change my life, getting high was the only lifestyle I knew. Without Christ to repair it, I wouldn't have known where to start. I asked Christ to take charge and fix me, but I had to seek His Kingdom first so all those things could be added to me (Matthew 6:33). I had to accept Christ as my Lord and Savior and apply my life to the Word of God by studying and living the life style of Christ and going to church instead of the crack house. I needed to start tithing and giving (Malachi 3) of offerings instead of giving my money to the kingdom of satan. From there, I watched God open the windows of heaven.

I'm now an active Deacon in my church, Provision of Grace World Missions Church in Philadelphia. The Lord placed me as chairman of his Drug and Alcohol Recovery Ministry. I am also an active street minister spreading the word of God, instead of a street addict telling others where to buy the best crack. The Lord has provided us with a luxurious apartment for the last eight years, instead of a garage or partially abandoned house. He also ensures that the bills are paid in full every month before they are due. Praise Jesus! I have a nice fully insured car for church, instead of a broken down bike with a flat tire to ride to the house of satan. Instead of putting my money into the hand of a dealer, I put it into the collection plate and watch the blessings overflow (Romans 5:10 For if, when we were enemies, we were reconciled to God by the death of His Son, much more, being reconciled, we shall be saved by his life). Remember, God added these services and things unto me for HIS Glory!

God placed it on my heart in 2003 to adopt a fine little girl that means so much to me, something I wouldn't have even considered before, but I was instructed and compelled by the spirit of God; to raise this particular child under the care of my wife and me for HIS purpose. This is one of the best tasks the Lord has assigned to me. Her name is Samarra Toni Love. We are raising her to love God with all her heart (Matthew 22:34-38), and it is such a pleasure to watch her clap her hands and dance in church praising the Lord. It overwhelms me to watch her because she was removed from a crack cocaine environment and was born addicted. She is now a healthy and happy child with this new life that Christ has given her.

I can take no glory for who God has made me. IT WAS NOT MY DOING, but a gift. He is the transformer to the image of His Son (John 1:12). This generation has never seen or physically walked with Jesus, that's why God has to supernaturally change us to what He wants us to be. He is the potter and we are the clay (Jeremiah 18:1-6 & Isaiah 64:8). Allow the potter to do his work in you. Through good times and hard times in your spiritual growth, the Lord has to remold the mess we and atan made of the clay. Sometimes the reshaping may hurt, but it will always turn out to be perfection. That can only happen if you allow Christ to do the molding by himself, while you're obeying the word of God (1 Peter 5:10 But the God of all Grace, who hath called us unto His eternal glory by Christ

Jesus, after that ye have suffered awhile, make you perfect, establish, strengthen, settle [you]). Remember, you must renew your mind (Romans 12:2) for God to transform you.

You must first believe in your heart that Jesus died and rose from the dead as the conqueror of life and death and shed His blood for the remission of sins, then you must dedicate your life to God through Jesus Christ and you can do so now by speaking this prayer aloud for salvation (Romans 10:9-10). "Father, I know I have sinned and I ask you to forgive me of all my sins. Cleanse me from all unrighteousness. I believe that Jesus died and rose again and I ask you for a new life in His name and for you to take full control and be the Lord of my life. Never remember my sins against me anymore and restore unto me a new spirit and lead me down the path you died for me travel. I thank you, in Jesus name I pray AMEN." You are now a new creature in Christ Jesus (Romans 10:9-10). Some people choose not to remember their past, which is okay. I chose to remember every detail of mine because it makes it harder for me to ever return to the compelling grip of the evil one and it allows me to give testimony to others about how far Christ has brought me.

For Centuries, people have tried to eliminate the word of God from the world and His influence on mankind. Kings, Pharaohs, presidents and princes have all tried to, and all have failed and died. The word of God lives on undefeated then, now and forever (Matthew 24:35). You can trust and stand on the Word, because we, as humans, may fail, but God's Word never fails (Isaiah 9:6-7). I was watching a talk show while writing this book and a world renowned psychic came on and said "There is no such thing as demons or the devil ...", but all along she continued to talk about God, who she claimed to believe in. The same Bible that talks about a living God, also talks about a living devil and demons. Satan is mentioned over 200 times in Scripture. The Bible wouldn't have even been written if there wasn't a living satan to turn us away from a living God (2nd Corinthians 11:13-15, Acts 10:38 & Ephesians 2:1-3). Satan blinds the mind of man from doing the will of God (2nd Corinthians 4:4). For example, satan uses people like the psychic on the talk show to tell us that he doesn't exist. Using people to deny his existence is one of the most powerful weapons satan uses. We are in spiritual warfare, which is what Christianity is all about. (2nd Corinthians 10:3-5 For though we walk in the flesh, we do not war after the flesh, for the weapons of our warfare [are] not carnal, but mighty through God to the pulling down of strongholds. Casting down imaginations, and every high thing that exalteth itself against the knowledge of God, and bringing into captivity every thought to the obedience of Christ). Ninety percent of the time, satan's attacks on people start in the mind, the other ten percent of the time shows in your actions. For example, think of a bank robber. The plan starts in the mind, which leads to the adamic nature of man and the deed is then sought out in his actions. It's the same with pornography, drugs, alcohol, or anything else the devil is planning, first in your mind, then in your actions. The word of God instructs us to put on the armor of God (Ephesians 6:11-

17 Put on the whole armor of God, that ye may be able to stand against the wiles of the devil. For we wrestle not against flesh and blood, but against principalities, against powers, against the rulers of the darkness of this world, against spiritual wickedness in high [places]. Wherefore take unto you the whole armor of God that ye may be able to withstand in the evil day, and having done all, to stand. Stand therefore, having your loins girt about with truth, and having on the breastplate of righteousness; and your feet shod with the preparation of the Gospel of peace: Above all, taking the shield of faith, wherewith ye shall be able to quench all the fiery dart of the wicked. And take the helmet of salvation, and the sword of the Spirit, which is the word of God).

What is the armor of God?

1. Loins girt with truth and wear the shield of truth which is the word ofGod.

2. The Breastplate of Righteousness is the belief and truth of the word of God and living according to it.

3. Living on the reality of the promise of Peace in your Christian Life because we serve the Prince of Peace.

4. Faith in the word and the promises of God to overcome principality and wickedness in your life, which are the number one repellants of your armor.

5. Your weapon is the word of God. That's the only thing to fight with in a spiritual warfare battle. Satan cannot be shot, spit on, cursed out or stabbed; you only have Gods word.

6. Praying without ceasing for guidance, and deliverance and giving thanks to God in all things (1st Thessalonians 5:17-18).

Remember, it says in Ephesians 6:11 that you must put on the armor. God supplies it, but you must put it on and He will spiritually teach you how to use it. God supplies the seed to the sower, but the sower must plant them, God supplies the worms for the birds, but they must go out and get them, and God supplies the Bible, but YOU MUST READ IT! James 1:22-25 says "Do not merely listen to the word and so deceive yourselves, do what it says. Anyone who listens to the word, but does not do what it says is like a man who looks at his face in the mirror and after looking at himself goes away and immediately forgets what he looks like. But the man who looks intently into the perfect law that gives freedom, and continues to do this not forgetting what he has heard but doing it, he will be blessed in what he does"

People, places, and things are still positive roles to obey as in secular recovery programs. Stay away from people you used to associate with when you were in your addiction (Blessed is the man that walketh not in the counsel of the ungodly, nor standeth in the way of sinners, not sitteth in the seat of the scornful Psalm 1:1). Places bring back negative memories and could allow people of negative influence to set you back to where you were or more likely worse off. Things also bring back negative memories. Stay away from pipes, match sulphur, alcohol or anything that reminds you of getting high.

The 12 Steps: Biblical Disciplines for Personal Growth

Living at Peace with God

1

Step 1 is about recognizing our brokenness. "For I have the desire to do what is good, but I cannot carry it out." Romans 7:17

1. We admitted we were powerless over _____, that our lives had become unmanageable

2

Step 2 is about the birth of faith in us. "If you have faith as small as a mustard seed, you can say this to the mountain 'Move from here to there' and it will move. Nothing will be impossible for you." Romans 17:20

2. Come to believe that a power greater than ourselves could restore us to sanity.

3

Step 3 involves a decision to let God be in charge of our lives. "If anyone chooses to do the will of God, he will find out whether my teaching comes from God" John 7:17

3. Made a decision to turn our will and our lives over to the care of God as we understood Him.

Living At Peace With Ourselves

4

Step 4 involves self examination. "Let us examine our ways and test them, and let us return to the Lord." Lamentations 3:40

4. Made a searching and fearless moral inventory of ourselves.

5

Step 5 is the discipline of confession. "Therefore confess your sins to each other and pray for each other so that you may be healed." James 5:16a

5. Admitted to God, to ourselves and to another human being the exact nature of our wrongs.

6

Step 6 is an inner transformation sometimes called repentance. "Humble yourselves before the Lord and he will lift you up." James 4:10

6. Were entirely ready to have God remove all these defects of character.

7

Step 7 involves the transformation or 'purification' of our character. "If we confess our sins, He is faithful and just to forgive us our sins and purify us from all unrighteousness." 1 John 1:9

7. Humbly asked Him to remove our shortcomings

Living in Peace With Others

8

Step 8 involves examining our relationships and preparing ourselves to make amends. "For a mans ways are in full view ofthe Lord and He examines all his paths." Proverbs 5:21

8. Made a list of all persons we had harmed and became willing to make amends to them all

9

Step 9 is the discipline of making amends. "Therefore if you are offering your gift at the altar and there remember that your brother has something against you, leave your gift there in front of the altar. First go and be reconciled to your brother, then come and offer your gift." Matthew 5:23-24

9. Made direct amends to such people whenever possible, except when doing so would injure them or others.

10

Step 10 is about growing grace-full relationships. "Continue to work out your salvation with fear and trembling, for it is God who works in you." Phil 2:12

10. Continued to take personal inventory and when we were wrong, promptly admitted it.

Growing In Peace

11

Step 11 involves the spiritual disciplines of prayer and meditation. "Is any one of you in trouble? He should pray" James 5:13 "Blessed is the man who delights in the law of the Lord, and on His law meditates day and night." Psalm 1:1-2

11. Sought through prayer and meditation to improve our conscious contact with God as we understood Him, praying only for knowledge of His will for us and the power to carry that out

12

Step 12 is about ministry. "Brothers, if someone is caught in a sin, you who are spiritual should restore him gently. But watch yourself, or you also may be tempted." Galatians 6:1

12. Having had a spiritual awakening as a result of these steps, we tried to carry this message to others, and to practice these principles in all our affairs.

A problem I had that hindered my recovery was that I blamed everyone else for what I allowed myself to get into. When I started accepting the blame myself, God was immediately able to work with me. Movies and music must be changed to give you a purer spirit. Music and negative television or movie viewing can pollute any Christians' spiritual growth. Knowingly sinning is a hindrance. James 4:17 says "To him that knoweth to do good and doeth it not to him it's sin!" (6 things God hates: A proud look, a lying tongue, hands that shed innocent blood, a heart that deviseth wicked imaginations, feet that be swift in running to mischief, a false witness that speaketh lies and he that soweth discord among brethren. Proverbs 6:17-19)

God is a holy God and hates sin. No sin will ever be tolerated in heaven, which is why we are to be remolded here on earth. A crack addict focuses on nothing but the next high. He doesn't even care about his own mothers' feelings. There was a time my mom purchased a video camera when they first became popular. She was so proud of that camera. One day my mom and dad went on vacation and she forgot to take it with her. I remembered it was in the house during one of my binges; I broke into my parents' first floor bathroom, took and pawned that recorder. It broke my moms' heart when she discovered it was missing. That incident bothered me so much, that a couple of years later, I bought her another one. I had a cousin suffering in his addiction so much that he would steal and sell anything that wasn't nailed down, even his newborn baby's formula. He told me once that he would go out and steal trash can lids, and then sell them door to door to get another hit. The most devastating part of the addiction for me was the tremendous remorse the next day. When I would think back on what I had done the night before and knowing I could never take it back, the spirit of suicide would creep in. There are people reading this right now in bondage to the enemy and feel that the enemy is God. GOD IS NOT THE ENEMY! The word of God says in John 3:16 "For God so loved the world that he gave his only Son that who so ever believe in him should not perish but have everlasting life." God gave us Jesus to save us from satan and ourselves, that is why we must give our lives back to Him!

In the Genesis 2:17, God knew Adam and Eve would disobey him and eat from the tree. In the N.I.V. version of the Bible, it says WHEN you eat of it, you will surely die, and the King James Version says the DAY you eat of it you will surely die. Adam and Eve did die that day as God had said they would. They died spiritually, not physically. A spiritual death is worse than a physical death, because a spiritual death causes you to lose your connection to God, you would be SPIRITUALLY DEAD. Jesus was sent for us to be reconnected to God through Christ and the Holy Spirit. The Bible says in John 3:3-7 "You must be born again it's a spiritual rebirth to come back into fellowship with God through Christ Jesus." Do you notice without Christ in your life how much rage you feel inside? No love for your fellow man, just self-centered needs, you have an 'all about me' mentality. Do you know why you feel hatred, envy, backstabbing, and talking about others? It is because you are separated from your Creator, which is God! Read Romans 1:28-32, it says that God has given you up, until sincere whole-hearted forgiveness is asked and you choose to come back into fellowship with Him (John 3:36). Another way to elevate your spiritual growth is to recognize our sin and come to the realization of who we are sinning against. Take your boss for example, if you were seated in the same office with your employer, would you pick up the computer off of the desk and walk out to your car and put it in your trunk without saying a word? If you were in a courtroom for a hearing, would you spit on the floor right in front of the judge? That is exactly the same way we go about our daily lives before the Judge of all Judges. God literally doesn't miss a heartbeat, he is omnipresent. God loves us, and just as our earthly fathers want the best for their children, so God wants the best for us too (Matthew 7:9-11). Our Lord knows we will sin sometimes unwillingly or make the wrong choice of words without thinking. The Bible says we all have sinned and fallen short of the glory of God (Romans 3:23). It also says that all men are liars (Psalms 116:11), Be Holy for I am Holy (1st Peter 1:15-16), Be perfect just as your father in Heaven is perfect (Matthew 5:48). God, our eternal Father is telling us to strive and reach for perfection through Christ Jesus our Lord.

Don't let the enemy tell you that you can't change because he will tell you that. The Bible says in 2nd Chronicles 7:14 "If my people that are called by my name, shall humble themselves and pray, and seek my face, and turn from there wicked ways, then I'll hear from heaven and will forgive your sin. Then I will heal their land." Now we will break this verse down. Ask yourself, am I called by Christ's name? The answer is yes because you are reading this book that was written for the glory of God in Christ's name. You must humble yourself by turning from your arrogance, pride and self centered ways. You must change to the mind of Christ, praying continually to God for renewal of your way of thinking and actions to please Him. Keep your mind and heart on Him, turn from the sinful things you used to do, then He will hear you on His throne and forgive all of the sins you have ever committed and change your whole way of life.

This was a verse that God presented to me early in my sanctification. Remember, God is faithful to his word, now you must remain faithful to him. I will mention again, FAITH is number one in your relationship with God. This is true because we are dealing with a Heavenly Father that is unseen. Creation speaks of His existence, for example, think of a tiny seed, when it is grown, this tiny thing produces food for us to eat and wood for us to make furniture, paper, and houses among other things. Think of the sun and how it heats the earth to make flowers and trees grow and a moon to give us light by night. It took intelligence to make a human being and provide them with the intelligence that we possess, also, the miracle of one human giving birth to another human. A computer is the most high tech device in the world. Now think of this, God gave us the knowledge to build it and the knowledge of what materials he made and placed in the ground for us to build it from.

The Bible speaks of this same subject in Romans 1:19-20. Harvard University said it would cost five trillion dollars for the parts to build a human body. Scientists say that creation came by way of the "Big Bang". Well, you must go beyond the "Big Bang" theory and ask yourself who caused the big bang? It was God, the Almighty! "In the beginning, God created the Heavens and earth" Genesis 1:1 then BANG! If there were a big explosion in the desert, somebody caused it, and that kind of explosion wouldn't produce anything but a big hole in the ground. This alone speaks of the reality and existence of God.

People wonder why there is so much evil, rape, suicide and sin in the world. I'm going to tell you why. Man has CHOSEN to separate himself from God and His Law. If you take the Ten Commandments and practice them, there would be no such thing as using God's name in vain, lying, fornication, stealing, disrespecting parents, or murder. Everyone would be going to church, and jails and penitentiaries would virtually go out of existence. All of this would come to pass if we wholeheartedly lived and practiced the Ten Commandments of the word of God. The first mistake was when the government took prayers out of the schools in 1963. Man insists on doing things his own way and all the things mentioned previously are the result of it, and it won't get better until we turn around and seek the kingdom of God (Matthew 6:33). Until then, there will be no love, joy or peace in this world which is the fruit of God's spirit (Galatians 5:22). Love, joy and peace are the nature of God, but not the nature of this world. The world can't give you these traits because they're NOT of this world, they're of God and only he can provide the genuine quality of His fruit, anything else is a false imitation.

God is love, and true love is not forced; God will not force his spirit on anyone. Forced love is not love. Forced love is of the devil, forced love is rape! We cannot save the world. The Ten Commandments have to start with the individual, it begins with you and you must let it through you; allow it to permeate your household, and from there, it can permeate the world. Let's talk about imitation love. Satan has showered this world with imitation love and it has given birth to fornication, homo-sexuality, pornography, drugs and alcohol. People in this world fall into those traps trying to fill the void that's only supposed to be filled with the love of God. False love is pacified for a while until it shows its ugly side. God' s love has no ugly side, it only festers, and festers desiring within yourself to want more and more of that spiritual high of the Holy Spirit until you can't get enough of God. Sin tries to work the same way in the same area within you, but it is an imitation. It makes you crave more sex, porn, drugs, alcohol, or whatever. It can't get enough which leads to destruction. God's addictions lead to life.

We are eternal spirit beings living in temporary human earthly bodies. The high spiritual COMMANDERS are God and the devil, which are eternal spirit beings without earthly bodies. We must choose whose spirit our spirit will be con-nected to. Our body is not who we are, who we really are is inside of us. It is unseen as our Heavenly Father is unseen. Absent from the body and present with God (2nd Corinthians 5:8). He knows us by our spirit connecting with his spirit and if it makes a negative contact, it would spark and cut itself off. Furthermore, since they did not think it worthwhile to retain the knowledge of God, he gave them over to a depraved mind; to do what ought not to be done. They have become filled with every kind of wickedness, evil, greed, and depravity. They are full of envy, murder, strife, deceit, and malice. They are gossip-ers, slanderers, God-haters, insolent, arrogant, and boastful; they invent ways of doing evil; they disobey their parents; they are senseless, faithless, heartless, and ruthless. Although they know God's righteous decree that those who do such things deserve death, they not only continue to do these very things but also approve of those who practice them. Romans 1:28-32. Our insides shows itself by our reactions and how we respond and do things. You can look at a depressed person and tell how their spirit is affecting them by their facial expressions, but it all starts on the inside, just as a happy spirit shows itself by smiles and laughter. The emotions are birthed from our soul.

What is your soul? Your soul is your mind, will, and emotions. Your spirit is your conscience or inner person. God and satan both speak to your spirit, learn to differ between the spirits. The Bible says that God's children obey His voice (Joshua 24:24) (John 10:27). Allow your spirit to learn the voice of God, which you can only do through the written word of God, which is the Bible, and by developing a personal relationship with Him through prayer, fellowship, communion, and worship. We have spent so long in a [personal relationship with the devil that we feel it is a normal way of life; IT ISN'T! We were created by a Holy God to be programmed in the body to live according to the perfect will of God. Anything else is deception.

Change is hard for some people even when it is a positive change. It's hard giving up the lifestyle of fornication, hanging out with the guys, drinking, bad language, negative secular music, and movies, but remember, these things are not of God, and we can never please God with such activities in our lives. NEVER! God says in his word that he is the same yesterday, today, and forever (Hebrews 13:8) which means his views and feelings toward sinful habits will always be the same. To him, sin is sin.

During the writing of this book in October of 2006, my youngest brother that I spoke of earlier has been in the hospital due to a swelling of his air passage in his neck. On October 9, our mother called me at 12:15 pm and requested that I come to the hospital because they had Rodney on life support. It shocked me tremendously because I was told he only had bronchitis. I immediately went to the hospital and after I arrived andpulled back the curtain surrounding his bed, I was stunned and horrified by what I saw. There was a lifeless body on the bed with tubes in his mouth and wires everywhere. I instantly began to weep, knowing it was the end of my baby brother. I just felt it was because of his lifestyle of drugs, alcohol and rebellion against God. He was going straight to Hell. The spirit of God immediately came over me and said "Tony, what are you doing? Get some water and anoint his head and pray." I looked for something to pour water into, but couldn't find anything so with shaking hands I picked up a surgical glove. I poured water into it, and held it up to God, then began to pour it on Rodney's head. I blessed my brothers' head and began to pray. The doctors had told me prior to my doing this that Rodney didn't have a heartbeat from the time he was found in his apartment until after he arrived at the hospital emergency room, which was at least 20-25 minutes due to having to carry him down from his 3rd floor apartment (the elevator was broken). They said it was a possibility that he had suffered brain damage due to lack of oxygen. I prayed to God through Jesus name and asked him to have mercy on Rodney. After praying and praying, God told me in my spirit loud and clear "I'm going to have mercy on him." With my mother looking on, I went to the other side of the bed so I could see his face, because I couldn't stand looking at him in the condition he was in. I could see color and life had reappeared in his face, so I called his name and he looked wide-eyed right in my eyes and I praised God in my spirit. I told him that our mother was there too, and he looked down for her. I pulled her by the hand to come closer to the bed and he followed her movements with his eyes. I later realized the Lord had mercy on my mom and me as well, because it would have been hard for us to not know the status of his brain activity. That blessing showed us that his brain was functioning and that he could understand me. The doctor said to our mother before I had arrived that he didn't know if Rodney would live or die.

Days later, the doctors said there was a cancerous tumor in Rodney's throat and he may never talk again, especially if they had to remove his voice box. I was able to accept that, at least he would be able to function in every other way. Then I thought about God, and the prayers that were being sent up for Rodney by my pastor, my rabbi friends, my brother Anderson, and a host of other believers, so I began to pray "Father, there is nothing to hard for my God. Restore Rodney's voice." On October 25, 2006 my mom called me and said "Rodney is talking!" He is now eating solid foods and standing for short periods of time, as well as professing the name of Jesus Christ. The doctors have also said that the tumor is non cancerous. He said to me on this day "I am forty-five years old and born again." God is still in the miracle making business. All praises, glory and honor is due God and our Savior Jesus Christ as we say thank you Holy Spirit.

Now Rodney has a new lease on life, but it is up to him to live his life in a Godly manner. There is an awesome spark in your spirit knowing you are living a true Christian life. You know you're saved, you're on your way to heaven and in God's grace, protected by his holy angels (Psalm 91:11). All of the drugs on earth can never give you a greater satisfaction in life. In my early Christian years, the Holy Spirit led me to read Matthew Chapters 5-8. I found this to be an excellent scripture reference for a new creature in Christ. It teaches you about living responsibly in the sight of God, how to pray, God's provisions, the do's and don'ts, and lining up your new life with the Word. Never seek a Christian life for things, a new car, house, spouse, or even for sobriety. Seek it for a relationship with God and because you love Him. Everything else will automatically come to be the way the Lord sees fit for your well being. You're his child and Father knows best. God knows that if you seek Him for material things, when you receive what you're looking for, you will leave Him. He knows our hearts and He responds by what's in our hearts, even when we ask Him for salvation. God knows us better than we know ourselves.

A person with a full head of hair has no idea how much hair they have, but God cares so much about us, that he numbered every one of our hairs (Matthew 10:30). This verse clearly tells us he knows us better than we know ourselves. When you comb or brush your hair and strands come out, he deducts them. There was a famous actor that decided to accept Christ on his death bed, and his words were "I'm looking for a loophole." If that was in his heart when he accepted Christ, he may have had a problem (I would say) when he stood before God. I had another cousin that was so overcome by satan and crack in the early eighties; he began to see evil spirits. I was told by his brother that he drank battery acid and ate broken glass and raw meat. He eventually hung himself; satan had deceived him until the end.

You, the reader, have a chance at a fresh start that can be made today if you turn your life over to the Savior of man and woman kind. I have no cravings and no urges. I was delivered! Just as the woman that was healed of the issue of blood (Luke 8:43-48), He took it away! Whomever the Son sets free is free indeed (John 8:36). We do not have to live this way any longer. Don't allow satan to tell you any differently. I was made a new creature and creation in Christ Jesus name. You can be too. Just have faith, trust Him, and give your life over to Him. I love you and may God bless you and yours

978-0-595-43985-0

0-595-43985-3

www.ingramcontent.com/pod-product-compliance
Lightning Source LLC
Chambersburg PA
CBHW050344290526
45785CB00006B/2624